Touching Lives,
One Song
at a Time

Jennifer Jonas

BALBOA.
PRESS

A DIVISION OF HAY HOUSE

Balboa Press books may be ordered through booksellers or by contacting:

Balboa Press
A Division of Hay House
1663 Liberty Drive
Bloomington, IN 47403
www.balboapress.com
1 (877) 407-4847

Because of the dynamic nature of the Internet, any web addresses or links contained in this book may have changed since publication and may no longer be valid. The views expressed in this work are solely those of the author and do not necessarily reflect the views of the publisher, and the publisher hereby disclaims any responsibility for them.

The author of this book does not dispense medical advice or prescribe the use of any technique as a form of treatment for physical, emotional, or medical problems without the advice of a physician, either directly or indirectly. The intent of the author is only to offer information of a general nature to help you in your quest for emotional and spiritual well-being. In the event you use any of the information in this book for yourself, which is your constitutional right, the author and the publisher assume no responsibility for your actions.

Scripture quotations marked KJV are from the Holy Bible, King James Version (Authorized Version). First published in 1611. Quoted from the KJV Classic Reference Bible, Copyright © 1983 by The Zondervan Corporation.

Print information available on the last page.

ISBN: 978-1-5043-7676-1 (sc)
ISBN: 978-1-5043-7678-5 (hc)
ISBN: 978-1-5043-7677-8 (e)

Library of Congress Control Number: 2017903985

Balboa Press rev. date: 03/18/2017

Dedication

I dedicate this book to my wonderful clients and their families, who have inspired me to be a better therapist and a better person. In touching their lives, they have touched mine.

Acknowledgments

A few years ago, I sat down with Dottie Coan to discuss an idea I had of writing a book about my therapy stories. I had been singing to Dottie's mother, Edna, at the time. She had seen firsthand the magical effect music had on her mom, so she agreed wholeheartedly that a book like this would be wonderful and beneficial. Her belief in me gave me the courage to begin writing.

Along the way, I asked for help from my literary friends: Marikay Tillet, Rosalind Fellwock, Mary Williamson, and Courtney Potts. They were there to check my grammar, cross my t's and dot my i's. I am extremely grateful to each of them.

I also want to thank my photographers for the touching photos of their loved ones that I used in this book. The pictures brought their stories to life! For their editing and touch ups, I thank Joe Matus and Ashley Justice.

The precious hands on the front cover of this book belong to Rosalind Fellwock and Cailey Moak, and the talented hands that took this touching photograph belong to my son, Jesse Akozbek.

Lastly, I need to thank all the family members of the clients I have sung to these twenty-five years. Your mother, your daughter, your husband, or your son touched my life in a profound way. It was my honor and privilege to sing to them. Thank you.

Contents

Preface

For twenty-five years, I have seen the magical effect music has on people in my work as a music therapist. It has been my adult dream to share my stories in a book that is made up of my most memorable moments working with my clients. Some memories are from my work with children, while others are from my work with seniors. Each story demonstrates how music can touch our lives in deep and profound ways—whether it is through reaching a person living with Alzheimer's disease, helping someone to die a more peaceful death, or inspiring a child with a special need to dance and sing! By sharing these stories, I hope to inspire the reader to sing to a loved one. Hearing a familiar song can be quite therapeutic to a child who is upset or a senior who is sad. In my experiences, I have found that sharing a familiar song not only touches the life of a loved one, but it also touches one's own life, for in giving, you shall receive.

Healing Tears

When I was studying music at the University of Western Ontario, I had the opportunity to visit my friend's mother in the hospital. This was the very first time I brought music to someone in a hospital setting. I had heard of music therapy but hadn't begun my own studies in the field yet. I brought my autoharp, for I had not yet learned how to play the guitar. It was near Christmas, so I also brought my favorite Christmas songs to play.

I must admit I felt a little strange walking through the halls with this autoharp in my arms, but I was greeted with a welcoming smile when my friend's mother, Mrs. Martin, saw me enter her room. I settled beside her bed and began with one of my favorite carols, "What Child is This," based on the "Greensleeves" melody. A few moments into the song, I noticed that Mrs. Martin was crying. I felt awful. I meant to bring joy to this dear woman, and I had made her cry! I stopped after that first verse and apologized for upsetting her. She immediately responded by saying, "Oh, Jennifer, I have wanted to cry for so long but have not been able to. Your music helped the tears come out. Thank you!"

It was then I understood that some tears need to be shed. These were healing tears for Mrs. Martin, and she felt much better for having shed them. I also understood that it is important for us not to push our feelings down and ignore them, but to let them come out in tears or in words.

I was able to continue singing Christmas carols to Mrs. Martin, and I felt relieved and happy to see the smile on her face. At one point, a nurse popped her head into the room and said that everyone in the hallway was enjoying the Christmas music so much, and would I please continue. I did, and I must admit I felt an inner joy. I was doing what I was meant to do. Later that evening, I left the hospital room with an assurance in my heart. I was going to become a music therapist!

A Waltz Remembered

During the time when I was studying music education in Canada, I began a sing-along program at one of the local nursing homes. All the seniors would gather in one room to sing their old favorites with me. This was a great time for me to learn all the songs from the early 1900s, songs like "By the Light of the Silvery Moon," "I Want a Girl (Just Like the Girl that Married Dear Old Dad)," "Let Me Call You Sweetheart," and "Pack Up Your Troubles in Your Old Kit-Bag." The senior residents were my best teachers, and with many songs, I learned wonderful stories of their past lives.

Along with the singing, we also danced. The waltz was the favorite dance for this group of seniors, so each week, I asked the gentlemen to dance a waltz with me. Now one particular gentleman named John had Parkinson's, and he shook quite badly. I was afraid to ask him to dance, but one day he approached me and asked if I would dance with him. I couldn't say no, so I quickly thought of the waltz song "When I Grow Too Old to Dream." As I began singing, we began moving to the waltz step with his hand in mine.

To my surprise, John stopped his shaking. He was able to move his feet to the 1-2-3 step and not tremble. He danced the whole song fluidly, and at the end of the song, he looked to me with tears in his eyes and said, "Jennifer, that was my wife's favorite song. Thank you." That moment, seeing his tears and his smile, I felt my heart touched to the core, and now I don't hesitate to dance with one of my Parkinson's residents if he asks me. After all, it may bring back an endearing memory of dancing with *his* wife.

Catharsis

After completing my music education degree in Canada, I followed my heart and continued with graduate studies in music therapy at Michigan State University. It was during my music therapy internship that I met one of the angriest clients I have ever had. He was a boy named Paul, and he lived in an institution. This was years ago, when people with a severe mental illness were institutionalized. Paul met with me once a week for a variety of music activities. On one particular day, when I was walking him to the therapy room, Paul was punching his hand and saying, "I want to break a window. I hate this place!" Well, I knew I had to postpone my planned therapy session and deal with his anger.

When we got to the music therapy room, I found the two biggest drums I had and the two biggest mallets. I told Paul to sit down and drum exactly as I was doing. I began hitting the drum hard and saying, "I hate this place. I hate this place!" At first Paul looked up at me with big, questioning eyes as if he thought I had gone crazy or something, but then he began hitting the drum, lightly at first. As I hit louder and louder, he let go of his apprehension and began to bang his drum louder and louder. With this drumming and vocalizing of "I hate this place!" a catharsis began. After about three minutes of very loud drumming, a hint of a smile appeared on Paul's face, and then this smile grew and grew until he was laughing.

I had taken Paul's anger and displaced it on the drum instead of a window or another person. Paul left that music therapy session much differently from the way he arrived. The next day, I inquired of his counselor how Paul was after our session. He answered, "Very well. Why do you ask?" I then explained the transformation that took place within Paul.

You see, music can take our anger, our frustrations, and our hurts, and diminish them to dust, which we can then just blow away; all we are left with are the sweet sounds of music and an inner peace.

The Wedding Song

With my master's degree and internship completed, I returned to Canada and started my first private practice in Toronto, Ontario. One of my contracts was with a local hospital, in their palliative care unit. I sang to each of the palliative care patients every week. Many of the patients had friends and family visit them, but James was one of our patients who never had any visitors.

Nobody came to the hospital to see him, so I went to his room one day and asked if I could be his friend and sing to him each week. James agreed, but he told me he wanted to hear only one song, and that was his wedding song. This song meant more to James than anything else, so each week I sat at his bedside, lifted my guitar, and sang "Ave Maria, gratia plena, Dominus tecum..."

"Ave Maria" was his beloved wedding song, but it was more than special to James, for every time I sang that song from beginning to end, the memory of that entire wedding day came vividly back to him. James recalled his wife's beautiful bouquet, her lacy white dress, and the sparkle in her eyes. He remembered his dark suit, how warm the day was, how happy he was, and many more images. Recalling these details brought him pleasure and joy, and these recollections made up our conversation each week.

If I was lucky, James would talk just a little about his wife and their only son. One day I asked what happened to them, and with a deep sadness, he told me they had both passed away, leaving him alone in the world. James wanted to die peacefully, and hearing his wedding song brought him this peace. So the week that he went into a coma, I continued to sit at his bedside and sing his beloved "Ave Maria." Maybe, even in his coma, he relived his wedding day once more.

Memories

A ll of my senior clients love to reminisce. The memories of their past lives are so important to them. They make up the fabric of who they truly are. So when I meet a senior client for the first time, I ask them to share a memory or two with me.

This is what I did when I met Ellen. On my first visit, the two of us sat down at her kitchen table, and we went through my songbook. Ellen picked out her favorites, and with each song, she had a little story to tell. "Johnny's So Long at the Fair" brought on a story about her husband because his name was Johnny. The song "When You Wore a Tulip" brought back memories of Ellen's garden full of springtime flowers. "Take Me Out to the Ballgame" reminded her of watching her dad play baseball on a warm summer night. She also recalled the times she was not allowed to go. When I asked her why not, she wrinkled her nose up and said, "Mother made me stay home and peel potatoes!" I laughed when she recalled that memory. "School Days" reminded Ellen of her elementary school years. Each time we sang that song, she liked to tell me, "You know, mother made us go to an all-girls school."

I loved hearing Ellen's stories as much as she loved telling them. After a year of therapy visits, I thought I'd heard all of them, but one afternoon, she surprised me with a new one. On this particular day in June, I was singing love songs. After I sang, "Let Me Call You Sweetheart," I asked her, "Who was your sweetheart, Ellen? Was it Johnny?"

She surprised me with her reply. "Oh no, it wasn't Johnny! It was Ozy!"

"Who was Ozy?" I asked, and Ellen, with a twinkle in her eye, said, "He was a boy I met after school!"

In the second year of my therapy visits, Ellen's health declined. She had more days of confusion and sadness. On Ellen's sad days, when she was anxious and worried, I sat with her and sang the songs that cheered her, the ones that brought back all her fond memories. On one occasion, I noticed Ellen looked troubled. I asked her what she was thinking about, and she replied, "I haven't seen my husband in a very long time."

I knew Johnny had died many years earlier, but I didn't say that out loud. Instead, I took her hand and asked very gently, "Is he in heaven, Ellen?"

She looked at me with big eyes and quickly said, "Well I hope so!" We both laughed, and after that, Ellen's mood changed. She was much happier, and so we carried on singing and reminiscing.

I continued to sing to Ellen until the last days of her life. Her strength had faded, so I needed to speak her memories aloud for her. The songs we had sung as duets for two years were now sung solo. What didn't fade in Ellen was the twinkle in her eye.

The Universal Language

In my work as a music therapist, I have come across a few occasions when my client could not speak any English. But here's the beauty of music: it transcends all language barriers. It *is* the universal language. "Amazing Grace" has the same melody whether you are singing it in Germany, Italy, or France. If I can't speak the language of my clients, then I can still sing to them.

One of my palliative care clients named Sue couldn't speak English, and she didn't have family close by to visit her, so she was often lonely. I came into her room one day with my guitar, hoping that I could make contact with her through the music. Before I began to sing, I looked directly at her and smiled. Then I lifted up my guitar and started singing song after song. I first tried folk songs, then popular songs, and then contemporary religious songs. As soon as I began singing "Kumbaya, my Lord, Kumbaya," her eyes lit up. I found a connection. She was so excited to hear something she knew that she clapped her hands and laughed. I laughed too and then made a gesture with my hands to show her I wanted her to sing along with me. I sang in English, and she sang in her own native language. It was a bilingual duet of "Kumbaya," and it left a big smile on both our faces. After discovering that Sue liked this style of music, I was able to find a few other songs that she recognized: "Do Lord, O Do Lord" and "He's Got the Whole World in His Hands."

I made sure I visited Sue each week. She was always eager to hear her favorite songs, especially "Kumbaya." I didn't speak the language of Sue's mind, but I did speak the language of her heart.

I Love You, You Love Me

As a music therapist in palliative care, it is important that I address the families' needs as well as the patients'. I remember one family I worked with that had two very young girls. When I visited their dad, who was dying, these two children were often playing and jumping around the room while their mom was sitting on the chair beside her husband's bed. Most days, she looked worn and sad.

I noticed over a period of a few visits that no one ever spoke words of love out loud to Dad. I also knew he was not going to live for many more weeks. I felt that it was important for the dad and the children, as well as Mom, to hear the words "I love you," so one day I gathered the children around me and asked them to sing a special song with me. I used the familiar Barney song, which all the children knew at that time, with the traditional "This Old Man" melody. I began to sing quietly, "I love you, you love me, we're a happy family," and then the girls joined in, "with a great big hug and a kiss from me to you. Won't you say you love me too?"

At the end of that song, the two girls gave their dad a big kiss and a hug, leaving him with a wonderful smile on his face. Mom too had a smile on her face and a few tears in her eyes. The family needed to hear these comforting words of love, and I used a song to initiate it. I'm certain this is a memory the mom will cherish for the rest of her life—the memory of hearing her children express their love to their dad for what could have been the very last time.

When Words Fail Us

R obert loved his sister, June, and he wanted to make her dying days more peaceful through music. He asked me to come each week to sing to her and her family. June was able to speak for only my first few visits, and after that, she went into a coma. Since hearing is the last sense to go, I continued to sing to her. The music touched the hearts of her family, especially her children and husband, Andrew.

One day when Andrew came without his children, he asked if I would sing "Annie's Song" to June. The lyrics of this song talk of love. This was one way Andrew could tell his wife he loved her. I remember clearly what happened when I sang that song. I stood back and began, "You fill up my senses like a night in the forest, like the mountains in springtime, like a walk in the rain." While I sang, Andrew leaned over and caressed June's hair. I created a special and intimate moment for husband and wife, so special that I felt as if I were intruding on something private, just for them alone.

On my next visit with June, a visitor named Anna arrived with flowers. Once she placed the flowers in a vase, she sat in a chair beside June and didn't say anything. There was an awkward silence until I invited her to sing "Edelweiss" with me. Anna immediately looked relieved to have something to do, and she knew and loved that particular song. She came right beside me as I started to play my guitar, and she followed along with the lyrics: "Edelweiss, Edelweiss, every morning you greet me. Small and white, clean and bright, you look happy to meet me." Again, the lyrics of the song spoke for this friend. She didn't have to find the right words to say when the song said it for her.

Words of love, words of friendship, were lost in the human's mouth but found in a song. Once sung, they were expressed more beautifully. I was the messenger for husband and friend. I sang the words they could not form.

Calming Jackson

Jackson's preschool teacher saw how music had a positive influence on him, so when his occupational therapy stopped, she recommended music therapy to his mother, Tami. Tami also found music to be effective when teaching Jackson his numbers and letters at home, so she was eager to try this music therapy with me. We set up his goals, and then I wrote a session plan where I included all of Jackson's favorite songs. To my surprise, Tami told me one of Jackson's favorite melodies was Beethoven's "Ode to Joy." Tami said she played it often at home, so he had grown quite attached to it. In fact, the "Ode to Joy" melody was able to calm Jackson any time he became upset.

I made sure to bring my recorder to each therapy session so I could play that calming melody. Jackson often pointed to the recorder when making a choice on what he wanted to do next. We began a routine where I would play part of the melody on the recorder and then stop, and Jackson would finish by humming the rest of the notes. Now, Jackson was only four at the time, so that was very impressive! Jackson's other favorite melody was "Twinkle, Twinkle, Little Star." I'd start that song on my recorder and, similarly, Jackson would hum the notes I left off. He was always right on key.

One day in class when I arrived to do the weekly music circle, Jackson was crying. Something upset him, and his cries turned to screams. The children and I had just sat down for music time on the rug, and I remember they looked to me questioningly, like, "What should we do?" Instead of singing my hello song, I began humming the "Ode to Joy" melody quite loudly. Some of the children tried to hum along. I realized they could help me, so I stopped humming and told the children, "We can help Jackson! Follow me and sing 'lah lah lah lah' on this song he loves." All fifteen children began singing "lah lah lah lah" with me, some on the melody, and some not. But the "Ode to Joy" theme was there, and Jackson heard it and stopped crying! He looked quite surprised, and I might even say delighted, to hear that comforting melody coming from his friends.

I was so proud of the children. Together we used music to help their fellow student. Singing seemed to work like magic in changing Jackson's cries to smiles.

At Peace

When I arrived on the palliative care unit that day, one nurse approached me and requested that I first visit Adam because he was going to die imminently. I entered the room quietly, with guitar in one hand and music folder in the other. Adam's wife, sister, and son were at his bedside. Initially, the look on their faces was one of anger because I had intruded into their private place of mourning, but after I offered the music, especially one particular song, they relaxed and smiled with welcome.

Very gently and with the quality of a lullaby, I began singing "Amazing grace, how sweet the sound, that saved a wretch like me." "Amazing Grace" was Adam's favorite hymn, and by singing this, it was like an offering of a special gift to him in the last hours of his life. As I sang that hymn, Adam's sister joined in with a soft voice. It was during the singing that everyone seemed to relax more, and the feelings of tension dissipated. With this one song, I had made a connection, and the family began to trust me. Then they made request after request, and with each song I sang, they shared a special memory of Adam's life. They reminisced in these musical moments, painting a picture of his life for me.

Near the end of this musical visit, Adam's wife asked for their wedding song, "Ave Maria." This last song left everyone in the room feeling more comforted and very much in touch with their emotions. I quietly left the room after singing this song, not wanting to break the mood of peace and tranquility. One hour later, Adam died. Within minutes, his family requested to see me. When I returned to the room, they greeted me with smiles and told me of Adam's peaceful death. "He just stopped breathing," explained his wife. "I think he heard your voice and was at peace."

Ben and Me

At the age of seventy-two, Ben was diagnosed with prostate cancer and needed to be hospitalized. When he was admitted to the palliative care unit, he did not suffer from pain because it was well controlled. What he did suffer from was lack of stimulation. For this reason, the staff felt music therapy would be beneficial in alleviating his restlessness. The first session with Ben proved to be extremely successful. He was very excited when I entered the room with my guitar and asked him if he would like to sing a song. I quickly found out that Johnny Cash was one of his favorite singers and "I Walk the Line" his all-time favorite song. So this became our theme song. We began and ended each and every session by singing this country song.

Ben had a unique and spirited way of singing. He sang with his whole body: raising his chest, swinging his arms, and tapping his feet. His energetic body and boisterous voice were quite contagious and always got everyone in the room involved, even the elderly man in the bed across from him, who was hard of hearing. But it didn't matter how many joined in; you could always hear Ben's voice above the rest, country twang and all.

During one of my visits, Ben asked for my recording, called *Reminiscence*. He wanted to play it when he was alone. He said the music would keep him company, and the familiar songs would cheer him. He also made a special request. He asked if we could record our own duets on a tape during the next visit because, he said, "We sound awfully good together." I agreed wholeheartedly, and Ben proceeded to call and ask his son to buy a blank tape for our recording. Ben was thrilled, and I must admit that I too felt an excited anticipation for our next therapy visit.

That next week when I came on the unit, I was thinking of the songs Ben and I would record together. In my excitement, I walked directly to his room, bypassing the nurses station where I normally go to find out about the patients and their status. I looked in Ben's room and found an empty bed. He had died.

I felt a pang of sadness. I wasn't ready for Ben to die. I would dearly miss singing "I Walk the Line" and making that recording of our duets. I would miss this man's boisterous singing and joyful laughter. After a few moments, I walked back to the nurses station. I asked one of the nurses about Ben's death. "He died peacefully," she said. "It was as if he knew he was going to die. He called his wife and told her he loved her, and then he turned on your tape and listened to the music. A few hours later, he died."

I'll Fly Away

I n 1998, my family moved to Huntsville, Alabama, and it was there that I met one of my oldest therapy clients. Edna was a dear, sweet lady of ninety-nine years. Edna had Alzheimer's, so she never remembered my name or what instrument I played. Each week was different: I was "the girl with the banjo," or "the girl with the fiddle." What she did remember was the happiness I brought her, and that was more important than my name.

Edna, like others living with Alzheimer's, did not live in the present. She lived in the memories of her childhood. I would use the old songs like "Working on the Railroad" and "Take Me Out to the Ballgame" to bring back these fond childhood memories. "Working on the Railroad" reminded Edna of one particular time she walked to the railroad to deliver her father his lunch. She had her brother's slingshot with her, and she remembered vividly how she shot her own thumbnail off when she let that stone go! "Take Me Out to the Ballgame" reminded her of going to the football games and how, on the cold nights, they would wrap their legs in paper bags just to keep warm.

The one aspect of the present that Edna seemed to be aware of was of her impending death. She wanted to hear her favorite hymns that talked of going to heaven, especially "I'll Fly Away." Edna wasn't a strong singer, but she made every effort to sing out on the lyrics "When I die, Hallelujah by and by, I'll fly away." It was even more joyful for Edna when her daughter, Dottie was there and sang along. Dottie made every effort to be there when I visited because, I think, it meant the world to her just seeing her mother happy, truly happy, in the music!

I remember my last visit with Edna. We were alone. As soon as I walked in the room, she looked at me and said, "Oh, we two are the winners. We are the winners!" I think "winners" meant the ones going home to heaven. Edna had walked her journey in life, and now she was ready to go home. On that day, she wanted to do only two things: sing "I'll Fly Away" and talk of her son, the one who had died young. She had a great excitement in her face as she talked of seeing her "sweet son." Thoughts of seeing him and of entering the gates of heaven brought happiness and peace to Edna in the last two days of her life, and then she flew away.

Child of Light

There are people who come into our lives and leave a deep imprint. Typically, it is an adult, someone older and wiser than ourselves, but I was touched by the life of one young child. Darby Jones was born eighteen years ago, and she came into my life because she had Down syndrome. I had the pleasure of being Darby's music therapist, and I knew right from the start that this girl was special! Darby had a twinkle in her eye that lit up every time she heard music.

Music was a gift to Darby. It inspired her to sing, to dance, and even to play the piano! It wasn't long before her parents signed her up for dancing lessons, and it was evident from the beginning that Darby loved to be on stage. She lit up the stage with those twinkling eyes and bright smile, yet she never took the limelight for herself. She always shared it with her peers. Whenever they felt nervous or scared, she always reassured them with, "Don't be afraid. It's okay. We can do this together."

Darby used this positive attitude to help in her fight against cancer—not once but three times. Darby endured countless days in the hospital, and on the darkest of days, Darby had a saying that kept her going. She would take in a deep breath and say, "Gray skies out; blue skies in. Gray skies out; blue skies in." Wow, such wise words coming from such a young child! She was an inspiration to all who knew her.

Darby's light touched the lives of so many, especially her parents, teachers, doctors, friends, and me, her music therapist, but that bright light went out in 2013. I had told myself that if I was ever asked to sing at Darby's funeral, I would have to sing "I Believe There Are Angels Among Us" because this girl surely was an angel on earth.

Darby's mother did ask me to sing, and she was touched that I chose this song, but she also requested that I sing the song Darby used to sing to her. I didn't know if I could make it through her song at the graveside, so I asked my daughter Emma to help me, and together we sang, "You are my sunshine, my only sunshine. You make me happy when skies are gray. You'll never know dear how much I love you. Please don't take my sunshine away."

Musical Midwife

A friend of mine once remarked that if we have midwives to bring souls into the world, then we should have midwives to help souls leave the world. As a music therapist in hospice, there have been many times when I have helped a precious soul leave our world. Let me tell you a story about how I acted as a musical midwife for JoAnn.

I was called by hospice to sing to JoAnn, and it was imperative that I go that day because she was not expected to live much longer. I met her husband, Hugo, and their son when I arrived. Immediately they took me to JoAnn's bedroom and then shared with me the songs they had chosen for her funeral. JoAnn was lying on her bed in a coma, unable to talk to me but very much able to hear all the songs I sang.

I started with one of the songs for the funeral, "On Eagle's Wings." I sang very strongly on the lyrics "And He will raise you up on eagle's wings, bear you on the breath of dawn, make you to shine like the sun, and hold you in the palm of His hand." I wanted to give strength to Hugo, who was singing quietly beside me with tears running down his cheeks. At the end of this song, Hugo shared with me how he and his wife sang in their church choir for years, he a baritone and JoAnn an alto. He had chosen all their favorite songs for her funeral to make it a testimony of her life.

I sang another song chosen for her funeral, "Be Not Afraid," and Hugo now joined in with a much stronger voice. I could see that he gained strength as he sang, "Be not afraid. I go before you always come follow Me, and I will give you rest." As Hugo sang, he held JoAnn's hand, letting her know he was with her. Their son, who was in the room, told me that he felt sure that his mother heard everything we sang. I could tell this brought him much comfort.

I returned the next two days at Hugo's insistence that his wife needed to hear the music to bring her peace before she left this world. But I think that Hugo also gained a deeper tranquility from singing these touching songs, songs that meant so much to them in their married life.

On that second day when I arrived, JoAnn had just passed away. Hugo didn't send me home but asked me to stay and sing over JoAnn's body. I entered the very quiet room where JoAnn's son and daughter sat looking fondly at their mother. As I prepared my music, JoAnn's priest was there to offer his blessing. When his blessing was done, I immediately began to sing "Ave Maria." There was such a peaceful stillness in the room as I sang. This spiritual song and the priest's blessing brought a holiness to JoAnn's death. It lifted her to the angels that were waiting to carry her soul home to heaven.

Take My Hand, Precious Lord

I had a dear hospice patient named Pearl, who lived in a teeny, tiny house in a teeny, tiny town in Alabama. When I went to visit her each week to sing her favorite hymns, I would leave my guitar case in my car so it would not take up too much space in the living room, where we sang. Pearl loved going to her church, but with her declining health, she was unable to go, so I brought the church to her by singing her favorite gospel hymns in her own living room.

Pearl had a sweet sister, Sarah, living with her, and she made quite an impression on me the first time we met. Sarah was small in stature, and she had the highest voice I've ever heard in a senior. On that first visit, Sarah requested "His Eye Is on the Sparrow," and then she sang along with me with the voice of a little girl. She had many childlike qualities that were quite endearing. For example, after we sang that hymn, Sarah clapped her hands, laughed, and said, "Ooo, sing another, sing another." Then she pulled me close to her forehead and said, "Oh I loves you! You are my angel!" Sarah was an inspiration to have in that room, but by my fourth visit, she was not in our therapy sessions because Pearl had grown weaker and needed to be in her bed. There was not enough room for the three of us in Pearl's bedroom.

Like Sarah, Pearl had many favorite gospel songs, but her two most loved songs were "I'll Fly Away" and "Take My Hand, Precious Lord." When I would sing these songs, Pearl would lift her hands to the sky and say, "Oh, Jesus, take me home!" Pearl took in the music like it was medicine to her soul, medicine that left her feeling uplifted, happy, and whole.

Pearl also had a favorite psalm from the Bible, Psalm 23. I would help her speak the psalm, "The Lord is my Shepherd; I shall not want..." and then I would sing it for her with a tune I learned growing up in my Lutheran church in Canada. I sometimes sang the Lord's Prayer as well, which helped Pearl feel as if she had been to church: hearing a prayer, reciting a psalm, and singing her favorite gospel tunes. Now she didn't feel so bad about not being able to go to her own church.

It wasn't long before Pearl had to leave her tiny home and move to a nursing home, where she could get the care she needed. A few weeks later, Sarah also moved to that home, and they were given beds side by side. It was nice, after all those years of living together, not to be separated, but to have each other so close. Sarah's health declined quickly, though, and within two weeks, she passed away. How Pearl missed her! She talked of Sarah going home to heaven in many of our next visits, especially when I sang "I'll Fly Away." She talked of Sarah flying home to heaven and that she would be coming soon.

Pearl stayed at that nursing home for quite a few months. Toward the end, she spoke of either going back to her tiny home or going to her eternal home in heaven. I was there every week to be a friend and therapist to Pearl. I sang her favorite hymns. She didn't want to hear anything else. On good days, she sat up in her bed and sang along with me. On days when she just didn't have enough energy, she stayed lying down as she listened to me sing her medicinal gospel songs.

My presence and the songs brought a smile to Pearl's face, and she always managed to say to me at the end of every visit, "Please pray for me; I loves you," and, "When are you coming back?"

As always, I reassured her, "I will always pray for you; I love you too," and, "I'll come back next week!"

I did come back to see Pearl each week, until the fall. By then, Pearl had returned to her tiny home. I'll never forget our last visit. I found Pearl in the living room, in a hospital bed that took up the space of the entire room. She was curled up in a fetal position, barely able to raise her head. I brought my guitar close to her, lowering my head to her face. After I sang "I'll Fly Away," I asked her if she was with me. She nodded her head *yes*. I knew which songs to continue with: "Amazing Grace," "Nobody Knows the Trouble I've Seen," and "Take My Hand, Precious Lord." I somehow knew this would be the last time I would sing to Pearl, so I took her hand and squeezed it tightly, telling her, "I love you Pearl. You are in my prayers." She didn't ask when I was coming back. We both knew she was going to her eternal home.

Transformation

Walking onto the skilled nursing floor where I work in Huntsville, Alabama, I recall feelings of helplessness that I had as a child when I used to visit my great aunt at a nursing home in Canada. Sad, blank faces looked back at me as I walked down the hall of that nursing home. I wanted to smile back at all those faces, but I felt a strange numbness in my heart, and I couldn't produce even half a smile.

Many years have gone by, and now I walk the hallways of the nursing homes in Huntsville with my guitar in hand and a big smile on my face because I know in a few minutes, I'm going to put life into those blank faces. I'm going to sing their favorite songs and spread joy where it is needed most!

When I get to the activities room, I notice that my group is assembled in a circle. Not everyone is awake, so I gently reach out my hand to touch those whose eyes are closed; and when they look at me, my eyes greet theirs with a warm smile.

I look around the room and notice that today my Shirley is crying. Her head is down, and she is whimpering words such as "I'm sad. I don't know what to do. I want to go home." I bring her wheelchair close to mine, and I start singing the song I know she loves: "Oh what a beautiful morning. Oh what a beautiful day. I've got a wonderful feeling..." and here Shirley joins in, "everything's going my way." Shirley knows all the words, and she continues with me on the first verse, "There's a bright golden haze on the meadow..."

The song is soon over, and with that last note sung, Shirley puts her head down and begins to weep again. I don't delay but begin singing one of her other favorites, "My Bonnie lies over the ocean, my Bonnie lies over the sea."

Within seconds, Shirley stops crying and begins singing along with me. In the middle of this song, Shirley looks up and smiles at me. She is so happy! She continues singing in her sweet high soprano voice and finishes the song, "Oh bring back my Bonnie to me."

My heart is not numb as it was years ago, but full of joy because I have taken Shirley's sadness and transformed it into happiness.

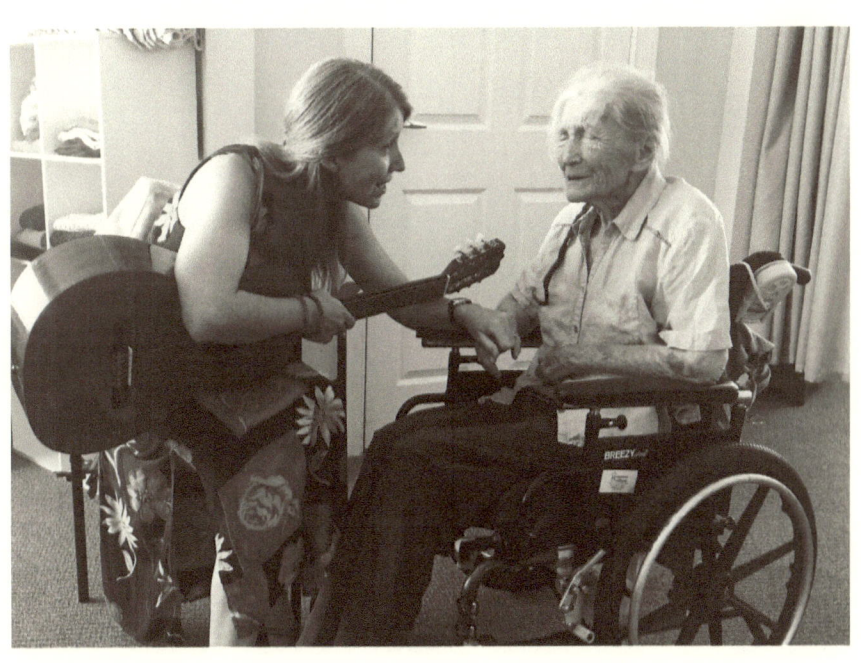

Mi-chael!

I started working with Michael in the fall a few years back. Michael has Down syndrome, and his mother felt that music therapy would help improve his speech. Since he loved music, it was a huge motivator for him. He loved to play the instruments and sing songs, but Michael's favorite activity was to dance! Michael and I would start our dance together, marching, jumping, and turning in circles. When that particular song was done, Michael wanted me to sit down and play my guitar while he danced his solo dance.

A large mirror was in the room where we did our therapy, so Michael would look at himself while he was dancing. Oh, he'd smile and laugh while he watched himself move his arms to the right and left, twirl, and even plie! The plie came from watching his sister dance at her ballet classes. While he danced, I would improvise a song: "Michael is dancing to the right and to the left. Oh, Michael is dancing, dancing all around!" Improvising the song allowed me to sing whatever Michael was doing at that moment. Hearing his name and having his very own song was extremely rewarding for Michael, and he was sure to bow at the end of his dance. I think the bow made him feel extra special!

Michael's mother had another goal for music therapy, and it was for him to say his name. She told me that he had never answered someone when asked, "What is your name?" But in December when he was at the doctor's office, a gentleman asked him for his name. This time he did answer "Mi-chael". Michael's mother was so overjoyed to hear her son say his name for the first time that she burst into tears. These were tears of joy! She believed that our music therapy sessions helped him learn how to speak his name—after all, we began and ended each session with singing his name. Hearing his name sung over and over, each syllable getting a note, gave him the confidence he needed to speak his name aloud.

So now when Michael is asked the question, "What is your name?" he does not pause to answer. These days we have a new goal in music therapy: to master all the words to Michael's all-time favorite song, "Jingle Bells!"

The Power of Music to Reach Within

Johanna has advanced Alzheimer's and has lost the ability to care for herself. She lives in a nursing home where someone else bathes, feeds, and clothes her. She no longer walks or talks but spends her days in her reclining chair. Her daughters wanted to offer her something special but struggled to find the right thing. Johanna's caregiver, Janet, heard one of my presentations on the power of music therapy and knew she'd found the right gift for Johanna. She spoke to the daughters, and they agreed to try this therapy; after all, their mother loved to sing and was in the Good Shepherd Church choir for years.

Janet joined me on that first offering of my music. I came prepared with the songs Johanna's daughters said were her favorites. When I began to sing the first song on my list, "Be Not Afraid," Johanna turned her head to the music coming from my guitar; and when the lyrics reached her, she began to smile. She recognized the words she'd sung in choir years ago. By the time I got to the chorus, she was tapping her foot on her chair and laughing. It was almost miraculous the change that occurred in her. She had gone from being totally unresponsive to being completely engaged in the music, *her music*. Janet looked to me with a great big smile. She had found what her daughters were looking for; a therapy to touch the heart of their mother, a therapy to reach into her world and make contact with the part of her that was still alive.

I sing to Johanna every week now, bringing my guitar and all her favorite songs. Sometimes I bring a drum or a bell for her to play. She needs my hands to guide and help her play the instruments. On a few occasions, Johanna has reached out as if in search of my own hand. I respond each time by putting my hand in hers. Then she will squeeze it or tap the rhythm of the song I'm singing. I feel a wonderful connection to her when this happens.

It is my goal, each time I visit, to reach Johanna wherever she is inside her mind. Some days it takes two or three songs, and other days it takes just one verse to bring out that genuine smile and that heartfelt laugh. Then I know I've reached her.

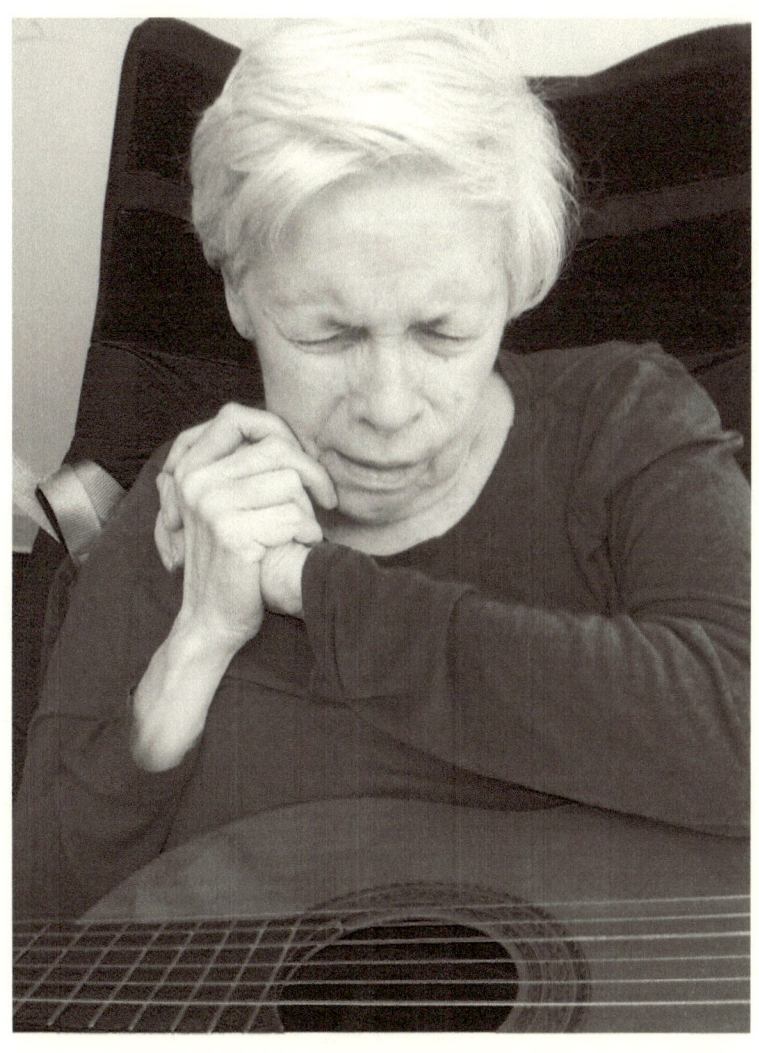

Doris Gives Hope

There are times in our lives when we doubt ourselves and our abilities, and ask the question, "Am I really making a difference in the lives of others? Am I really helping?" When I was on my way to meet Doris Bentley for the first time, this is what was going through my head: Was I helping the clients that I'd sung to all these years? Was I really making a positive difference? So I went to that visit with a heavy heart.

At the house, I was greeted by a caregiver and brought over to Doris, who was dressed very smartly and sitting in her favorite reclining chair. She greeted me with smiles and welcomed the first hymn I suggested, but before we could start, another visitor arrived, so I waited for him to greet Doris and then sit down.

When I began to sing that first hymn, "I Come to the Garden Alone," everybody in the room stopped and listened. Doris's eyes lit up as she recalled the words to that hymn. It was a hymn that she used to sing as a solo herself many years ago. By the time we'd finished the hymn, Doris's son and daughter arrived. She now had an audience, and I think she enjoyed singing to them. They all looked at Doris as she sang with me. There were tears in some of their eyes as they saw someone they dearly loved, singing, smiling, and experiencing joy. I continued asking Doris which hymns were her favorites, and then I invited her to sing them all with me. She had the strength to sing through some but not all of them. I gave her a voice where she had none and finished each hymn for her.

Doris not only sang, but she shared stories about when she was growing up with many of the hymns. This happens with all my clients because familiar music triggers our memories. Hearing a certain melody can bring back a memory so vivid that it's as if you were experiencing it once again. It was like that for Doris when she sang "The Garden Song." She remembered standing up in front of her whole congregation and singing her solo with a few butterflies in her stomach. As Doris recalled that memory, she had a joyful expression on her face. It was a fond memory and one that brought feelings of happiness and comfort. As a therapist, it is my job to find those familiar songs and sing them, as I'd done for Doris that day.

If I had doubted my worth and value as a music therapist, I only had to look at Doris and her children to see that I indeed was making a positive difference. I brought peace not only to Doris, but to her children and friend as well.

Hope with a Musical Sound

On a morning in January of 2013, Ronnie experienced a stroke. He lay in his garage as the blood filled his brain, and it wasn't until four hours later that surgery began. Ronnie suffered terribly from this stroke, and doctors told his wife, Lindy, that they had two choices: one, to perform a very risky operation where there was a high chance he would not survive, or two, put him in a nursing home and not expect anything from him. Lindy refused to accept either choice!

Ronnie had lost his speech, and he had lost his ability to care for himself, so Lindy took over. Despite the doctors' predictions, Lindy had hope. She got him into a speech therapy program at the local university and also into an occupational therapy program to regain his ability to perform daily tasks. It wasn't until a year and a half later that a dear friend of hers, Kathy, told her about a music therapist she knew who might be able to help.

That's where I come into the story. Lindy e-mailed me and asked if I could help! "Yes," I replied with enthusiasm! I'd researched a method called Melodic Intonation Therapy (MIT) where stroke victims suffering from aphasia or loss of speech can regain their speech through the singing of familiar songs. So we arranged our first meeting.

I met with Lindy and Ronnie at their Baptist church. After our greetings, we went to a quiet room where we wouldn't be disturbed. I pulled out my songbook, and with Ronnie's help, found eight of his favorite songs. I suggested that we start with "Amazing Grace." As I strummed the first chord on my guitar, Ronnie looked at me with big, questioning eyes, and then he took a deep breath and just started singing! He sang along with me, stumbling on a few words but making his way through the whole first verse.

Lindy was mesmerized. As she watched her husband sing, the tears welled up in her eyes. She got up and said she had to use the restroom, but later she told me she had to leave the room just to cry. Lindy cried tears of joy. She felt a reassurance of the hope she once clung to. Ronnie and I continued to sing his other favorites: "At the Cross," "Bind Us Together Lord," and "Give Me Oil in My Lamp." He struggled on the second verses, so I told him we would only sing the more familiar first verses and the refrains.

I thought I would try this MIT therapy technique with Ronnie next since he was doing so well. I told him we'd take out the lyrics to "Bind Us Together Lord" and replace them with conversational speech, such as, "Hello, how are you?" Instead of singing the words "Bind us together, Lord, bind us together, Lord," we sang "Hello, how are you? Hello, how are you?" To my delight, Ronnie did it! He sang a little slow and with broken syllables, but he did it.

After hearing him sing these new lyrics, Lindy made the comment, "Oh this is a keeper! This music therapy is a keeper." What I found most uplifting from this first therapy visit was the feeling of hope. I gave hope back to Lindy and, more important, to Ronnie.

A Musical Redirection

If you've ever worked with seniors living with Alzheimer's, you know that the dynamics of a group are critical. For example, if you put certain seniors side by side, a warm, friendly conversation may begin. But change that to another senior with a different temperament, and sparks may fly! This is where the caregivers are essential in helping to produce the best group dynamics possible.

I have a wonderful set of caregivers that I meet with every week at a daycare program for seniors with Alzheimer's. On one particular Friday, I felt tension in the air as soon as I arrived. There were two new seniors, and the energy they gave off was strong. John was very talkative and positive while Mary was also talkative but more negative in her energy. She took the instrument I gave her and waved it above her head like she was going to throw it at me. I didn't feed into her excitement but walked away to the other seniors in the group, greeting them with smiles and hugs.

Then I started with my traditional opening song, "You Are My Sunshine," and began to relieve some of the tension in the room. Smiles soon took over the faces of the twenty seniors sitting in the circle. I moved on to songs from World War I and II as the caregivers switched from instruments to balls to weights. Now this simple act of taking away an instrument or weight can pose challenges, and on this day, one senior became verbally aggressive. After her weights were taken, Jean began to yell, "Bring back my weights!" Everyone stopped and looked at her while she continued, "You have no right. Bring back my weights." Two of the caregivers went to her, bent over, and tried to calm her. I watched and noticed that Jean was escalating in her anger and frustration, and as she kept saying, "Bring back my weights to me," something clicked in my brain! I knew a song with those words. Take out just one word, and I could transform her words of anger into a song!

I jumped up, walked to the center of the circle, and began singing, "Bring back, bring back, oh bring back my *Bonnie* to me." Jean looked at me, and her eyes widened. I gave her a smile and continued singing, "My Bonnie lies over the ocean. My Bonnie lies over the sea..." All the seniors except Jean joined in singing, and with each passing verse, the tension dissipated. My goal was to keep Jean's gaze on me and shift her emotions. Thank goodness I know an extra few verses to this song, so I kept singing until a smile appeared on her face. And it did come. After the third verse, Jean's muscles in her face relaxed, and she had a calmer expression. In this case, I believe words did not help. It was the music that made the difference. Something as simple as the song "My Bonnie" redirected feelings of anger to feelings of calm, maybe even happiness.

Extra Special

L aura Beth was born on February 17, 1999, with an extra chromosome. That extra chromosome caused some delays, but that didn't stop her parents from signing her up for every class that her peers were in. Her earliest class was with me at the Infant and Toddler Program. When I started with Laura Beth, her goals at age two were to improve speech and fine and gross motor skills. We sang favorites like "Twinkle, Twinkle, Little Star" and "Itsy Bitsy Spider" while tapping the beat on the lollipop drum. We also tapped rhythm sticks together while saying favorite rhymes, such as, "Jack and Jill went up the hill," and "One, two, buckle my shoe."

These early musical beginnings prepared Laura Beth for success. As soon as she turned four, her parents enrolled her in figure skating lessons, then dancing, and then horseback riding! Once she reached school age, her parents made sure she was in a regular classroom, that she had an updated IEP (individualized education plan), and that her goals were being met. In elementary school, Laura Beth took up the cello and then the baton, taking lessons that were offered after school. In middle school, she joined the choir—the regular choir. I helped her learn her soprano part and was so very proud to see her up on stage with her peers at every concert.

Now in high school, Laura Beth is still taking choir because singing is her passion! She is part of the mixed choir (boys and girls), taking on challenging pieces, singing in Latin, French, Spanish, and any other language the director chooses! Together, we review all the lyrics and notes before the concert so she is prepared.

After working hard on some challenging lyrics, Laura Beth likes to sing one of her favorite songs, but before she starts to sing, she gets her microphone. Holding the mic, like they do on *The Voice*, makes her feel like a star. I give her the introduction, and she begins, "Imagine there's no heaven; it's easy if you try." She comes to the end of this Beatles song, "And the world will live as one," and there are tears in her eyes. I give her a hug and ask her why she's crying. She rubs her eyes, smiles, and says, "Ms. Jenny, I have happy tears."

Laura Beth works hard at all she does. She takes on every challenge, and one of her best rewards is receiving a medal. She received her first medal in 2008, at the Southeast Region Special Olympics ice skating competition. Of course, it was gold; that is her favorite kind of medal. Over the years, she has won many gold medals, but she is up for the biggest medal of her life. Laura Beth has been chosen to represent the United States in the winter Special Olympics in Austria! Nothing has ever stopped this girl, especially something as small as an extra chromosome. In my opinion, that extra chromosome has made Laura Beth extra special!

Edith's World

I could write a story for every time I sing at the nursing home—a story of how I touched some dear senior's life by the simple singing of a favorite song. Seeing their eyes light up with the recognition of a past memory is a delight I receive each time I go.

One of my dear seniors is sometimes hard to reach. Her name is Edith. She is an eighty-nine-year-old lady living with Alzheimer's. During my last visit with Edith, I placed myself right in front of her. I took her hands in mine, and then I looked deep into her eyes to make contact with her where she was in her mind. Once she looked at me, I started to sing, "Amazing grace, how sweet the sound." Her eyes widened with the instant recognition of the well-loved lyrics, and a slight smile appeared on her face. I moved my hands to the strings on my guitar to continue playing the hymn. The music coming from the guitar and my voice kept Edith alert and present with me. She stayed connected with me for the entire hymn, and by the end, she had tears in her eyes. I had reached her.

To keep her with me, I continued with another of her favorites, "You Are My Sunshine." As soon as I started this song, Edith swung her arms back and forth as though she were conducting me. I followed her beat, and then at the end of the song, she reached out, took my hands, and pressed them to her lips to give me a kiss. She never had to thank me with spoken words because she expressed it so clearly with that kiss and the sparkle in her eyes.

In the simple sharing of these two songs, I gave Edith a moment of joy, a feeling I believe she carried with her throughout that day. In her receiving of this joy, I, in turn, was given a gift: the gift of love.

Unmissed Opportunities

A nnelie was a little late coming to my music therapy group because she had been getting her hair done at the salon downstairs in the nursing home. When she arrived, the caregiver wheeled her into the room and set her in the back, a little outside of the circle. I finished the song I had been singing and wondered to myself if I should go over to Annelie. Her eyes were closed, and her head was down. She looked tired, and I didn't know if she would even respond to the music, but I decided to give it a try. I walked over to her wheelchair, knelt down so that my gaze was eye-level with hers, and began singing. Annelie was born in Germany, so I have found that singing her favorite German songs made the strongest, most positive impact on her. Today I chose to sing "Stille Nacht" (Silent Night), even though it was January. As I sang "Stille Nacht, heilige Nacht, alles schlaft, einsam wacht," Annelie raised her head, and then she opened her eyes and looked at me. The familiar tune reached her ears and produced a smile. With the little amount of energy Annelie had in her, she sang along with me for the rest of the song. I felt a warmth creep into my heart from the look on Annelie's face. Her eyes said, "Thank you! Thank you for leaving the circle and coming over to me to sing a song I love."

Two days later, I got a call from the activity director at the nursing home. She called to say Annelie had passed away. She also told me that she informed Annelie's children about how I had sung to her in German and how Annelie smiled and sang along. I am sure it touched their hearts to know that their mother experienced moments of happiness before she died.

After I said good-bye to the activity director, I came to a sudden realization: I must never question myself or wonder, "Should I bother to try?" If I had not taken the opportunity to sing to Annelie during that last music circle, then I would not have been given another chance.

Let us not miss the opportunities that we are given: opportunities to brighten up someone else's life, be it through singing a favorite song or through simply holding a hand or offering a heartfelt smile. You will be glad you did. I know I am.

Pure Joy!

My work is extremely gratifying, as you can imagine from all the stories I've shared here with you. I feel I have a perfect balance in my work as a music therapist, with half my clients being very young, and the other half very old. I enjoy sitting on the floor with my babies, singing "The Itsy Bitsy Spider," and sitting in my chair with my seniors, singing "You Are My Sunshine." By singing all their favorite songs, I can put big smiles on their faces, no matter what kind of day they're having. My babies may be teething, my seniors may be depressed, but the pain and sadness are washed away when the music starts.

What a joy it is for me each week to be the creator of smiles and laughter. My children and seniors don't know it, but I am working on real goals with them. For the children, my goals might be improving their communication skills, improving fine and gross motor movements, or improving social interaction skills, while for my seniors, my goals are different. Their goals may be to provide reality orientation, to reduce anxiety and depression, to reminisce, and most important, to create positive feelings and emotions.

My work is most rewarding when I make a positive difference with one of my clients who is particularly angry or sad, like the story I wrote about Shirley called "Transformation," or the story I wrote about Jackson called "Calming Jackson." These stories describe the wonderful, even magical, change that occurred through the music. Shirley went from weeping to singing, while Jackson went from screaming to smiling.

I have seen many magical moments throughout my twenty-five years of music therapy work; the magic of a child's first step while I sang my marching song or the magic of a child saying his name for the first time. I have seen the magic of a light going on in the eyes of my patient living with Alzheimer's while I sang her favorite hymn and the magic of a perfectly danced waltz with one of my Parkinson's patients while I sang a familiar tune.

Through the years, I have captured some of these magical moments in photographs, and I have shared them here in my book. The last photograph I have to share is one of sweet Emma dancing beside me. It's the Christmas program, and Emma has waited patiently for her favorite part to begin: dancing with Ms. Jenny! Her mom captured this photo at the perfect moment. The expression on her face is one of pure joy, an expression I have seen countless times on the faces of my clients over these twenty-five years.

In Closing

I t is my sincere wish that you have been inspired by the stories presented here to sing to a loved one. Sharing a song, without being worried about the quality of your voice, will be a gift to the receiver of that song. Now I know a lot of you will insist, "No, I cannot sing," but I believe we all have a song within us. It might be a simple song, such as "Twinkle, Twinkle, Little Star" or "You Are My Sunshine," but I guarantee that song will put a smile on someone's face, be it your mother, or your baby, or your best friend.

Someone as close to you as your mother or your friend will not criticize you for hitting a wrong note. Your baby will not wince and cry because you did not sing it perfectly. They will be happy that you shared a part of yourself with them.

For those of you who still insist, "I really cannot sing," I say to you: read a story (children love stories) or recall an important memory (seniors love to reminisce). I believe it is the act of just being present that is most important. Being truly present in the moment and not thinking about what you need to get done or what text is coming from your cell phone, that is the key.

When you share this song, this story, or this memory with your loved one, you will feel blessed. I believe it is in the act of giving that you will feel most fulfilled. Believe in yourself and your ability to make a positive difference in the lives of others. If we only try, we will make this world a better place!

About the Author

Jennifer Jonas is an accredited music therapist with over twenty-five years of experience working with young children and seniors. She began her music studies in her home country of Canada and then pursued her graduate studies at Michigan State University. Jennifer returned to Toronto, where she set up her first private practice. It was there she made her professional recording *Reminiscence*, featuring songs from her work in palliative care. In Toronto, she was interviewed by Peter Downie, longtime host of CBC TV and radio, and featured in his book called *Healers at Work*. In 1998, Jennifer's family moved to Huntsville, Alabama, where she continued her music therapy work with children and seniors. In 2013, she began sharing her music therapy stories on her local classical radio station, WLRH. She is a regular contributor to the *Sundial Writers* program. Sharing her stories on the radio inspired her to fulfill a dream of writing her own book, *Touching Lives One Song at a Time*.